My First Transportation Books

CARS GO!

Miranda Kelly

TABLE OF CONTENTS

A Crabtree Seedlings Book

Cars

Cars take us where we want to go.

My family has a car.

We **drive** to the store for food.

We drive to school and to work.

We drive to visit family.

ZG 6389 GD
HR

Cars have **lights** so that we can drive at night.

Slow

Cars can go slow or fast.

Fast

Always wear a **seat belt** in the car!

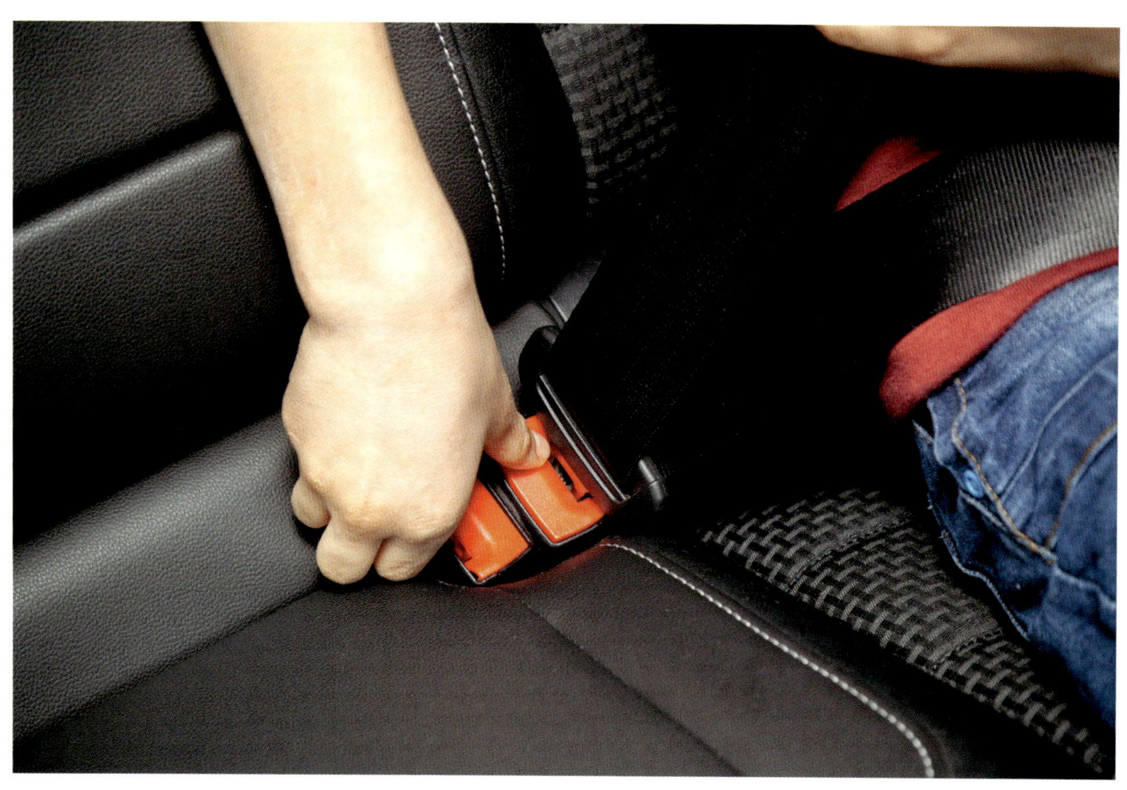

OG 531-E

Seat belts keep you safe.

Drivers must follow the **rules** of the road.

STOP
15%

Glossary

drive (DRIVE): To drive is to operate and control a vehicle.

lights (LITES): Lights are objects that give out light. People use lights so that they can see better when it is dark.

rules (ROOLZ): Rules are important instructions that tell you what you must or must not do.

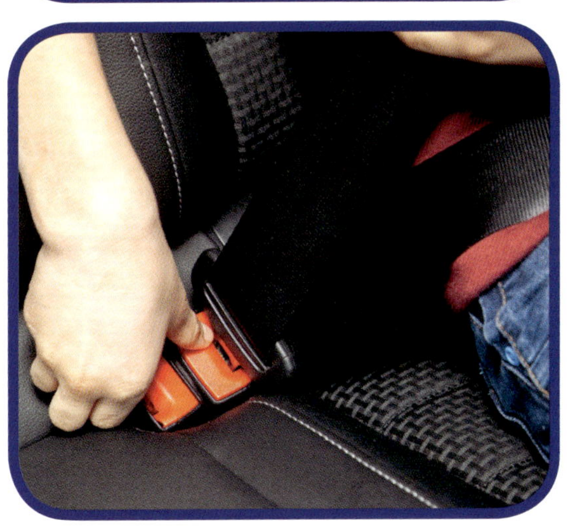

seat belt (SEET BELT): A seat belt is a strap that holds people safely in their seat.

Index

School-to-Home Support for Caregivers and Teachers

This book helps children grow by letting them practice reading. Here are a few guiding questions to help the reader build his or her comprehension skills. Possible answers appear here in red.

Before Reading

- **What do I think this book is about?** I think this book is about how fast cars can go. I think this book will explain details about how cars are made.
- **What do I want to learn about this topic?** I want to learn how fast the fastest car can go. I want to learn how old I must be to drive a car.

During Reading

- **I wonder why...** I wonder why cars have lights in the front and in the back. I wonder why I always have to wear a seat belt in the car.
- **What have I learned so far?** I have learned that drivers must follow the rules of the road. I have learned that seat belts are straps that hold people safely in their seats.

After Reading

- **What details did I learn about this topic?** I have learned that sometimes cars go fast and sometimes slow. I have learned that cars have lights so that the driver can see better when it is dark.
- **Read the book again and look for the glossary words.** I see the word *lights* on page 13, and the word *rules* on page 20. The other glossary words are found on pages 22 and 23.

Library and Archives Canada Cataloguing in Publication

Available at the Library and Archives Canada

Library of Congress Cataloging-in-Publication Data

Available at the Library of Congress

Crabtree Publishing Company
www.crabtreebooks.com 1–800–387–7650
Print book version produced jointly with Blue Door Education in 2023

Written by: Miranda Kelly
Print coordinator: Katherine Berti
Printed in the U.S.A./072022/CG20220201

PHOTO CREDITS:
Cover and title page: © Ivan Kurmyshov, pages 2-3 and page 14 © e2dan, page 4 © India Picture, page 5, 8 © Africa Studio, page 6 © Solomiya Malovana, page 7 © Hal_P, page 9 © zoff, page 10 © Tom Wang; Page 11 © ESB Professional, pages 12-13 and 17 © Goran Jakus Photography, page 15 © kurmyshov, Page 16: shutterstock.com/ Tomislav Pinter. pages 18-19 © Robert Crum, page 20 © Tyler Olson, page 21 © 2DAssets. All photos from www.Shutterstock.com except pages 12-13 and 17 © Goran Jakus Photography/istockphoto, page 15 © kurmyshov/istockphoto

Published in the United States
Crabtree Publishing
347 Fifth Ave.
Suite 1402-145
New York, NY 10016

Published in Canada
Crabtree Publishing
616 Welland Ave.
St. Catharines, Ontario
L2M 5V6